instant HARMONICA

By PATRICK BYRNE

QUICK AND EASY INSTRUCTION FOR THE BEGINNER

INSTANT HARMONICA

By PATRICK BYRNE

QUICK AND EASY INSTRUCTION FOR THE BEGINNER

Hal Leonard Publishing Corporation

7777 West Bluemound Road P.O. Box 13819 Milwaukee, WI 53213

E-Z Play ® TODAY Music Notation © 1975 HAL LEONARD PUBLISHING CORPORATION
Copyright © 1993 by HAL LEONARD PUBLISHING CORPORATION
International Copyright Secured   All Rights Reserved

HAVE FUN FAST!

Instant Harmonica is a totally new way of teaching yourself to play the harmonica in as short a time as possible. Yes, even if you have never played a note of music before in your life, you'll be playing your first songs on the harmonica in a matter of minutes. And what songs you'll be learning to play! We've chosen the best Country, Folk, and Cowboy songs around to insure that *Instant Harmonica* is not only fast but also a lot of fun!

Instant Harmonica will work with any ten-hole, diatonic harmonica.

CONTENTS

PLAYING AROUND

BE NICE TO YOUR HARMONICA

The harmonica is tiny compared to a piano or even a guitar, but it is still a true musical instrument that needs to be handled with some care in order for it to sound its best. First of all, don't expose it to things that you wouldn't like to be exposed to yourself such as excessive moisture, heat or cold. Try to resist the temptation to play in the shower, use that time to work on your singing.

HARMONICA HYGIENE

With *Instant Harmonica* there is little chance that your harmonica will sit around collecting dust. On those rare occasions when you are forced to stop playing due to hunger, lack of sleep, or the need to earn a living put your harmonica away in a safe, clean place such as a box, bag, or drawer. The emphasis here is on *clean* since whatever is on or in your harmonica will eventually end up on your lips or in your mouth. Remember, for harmonica hygiene, keep it clean!

HOW TO AVOID SOUNDING ALL WET

When you play your harmonica some moisture from your mouth (a.k.a. spit) will end up inside of it. This is unavoidable. If llowed to accumulate this will begin to clog the reeds, and the beautiful sound of your harmonica will go down the drain. When your harmonica's humidity starts rising, *gently* tap it against something that is firm yet soft like your hand or thigh. This will shake out most of the spit. It's hard to say how often you'll have to do this. Some people only do it every once in awhile while others can't seem to get through a song without taking a spit break. When in doubt, just do it. Your harmonica can never be too dry.

HOW TO AVOID GETTING BUGGED

Needless to say, you should avoid eating or drinking, especially anything that is sugary, just before or while you are playing your harmonica. Tapping will eliminate most of your spit with evaporation drying up the last few drops, but food particles and any sticky residue from your spit will remain inside your harmonica just about forever. The result will be a happy haven for creepy insects and foul odors. Unless you see playing the harmonica as a way to add to your bug collection, limit those between-song snacks.

HOLDING YOUR HARMONICA

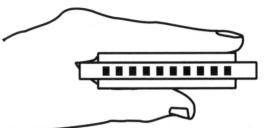

Hold the harmonica between your thumb and index finger. Right-handed players use your left hand, left-handed players use your right hand. If your harmonica has numbers, they should be on top of the instrument when you hold it in the proper playing position.

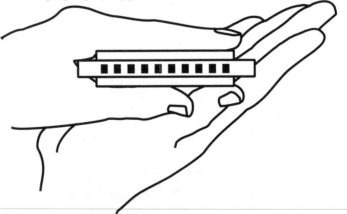

Your other hand supports the first as it covers the bottom of the harmonica. Be sure that your palms are touching.

MAKING A SOUND

By now you have probably made some sounds with your harmonica. If not, try some now and you'll hear how very easy it is to get a sound. Just gently *blow* air into and then *draw* it out of one or more of the ten small holes.

HOW IT WORKS

Inside each of these holes there are two tiny reeds: one reed is attached to the top of the hole and the other reed to the bottom. These tiny pieces of metal are the heart of your harmonica. When you blow into a hole, the bottom reed vibrates, and when you draw air through a hole the top reed vibrates. These vibrations in turn make the air around the reeds vibrate creating sound waves. These waves are what your ears hear as the sound of the harmonica.

Each reed is a different length (ranging from about a half inch to a quarter inch). The longer the reed, the slower the vibrations and the lower it will sound. When you play the harmonica the holes with the lower sounding reeds should always be on the left. Play the holes moving from left to right, and you should hear that each hole produces a higher tone. Try it!

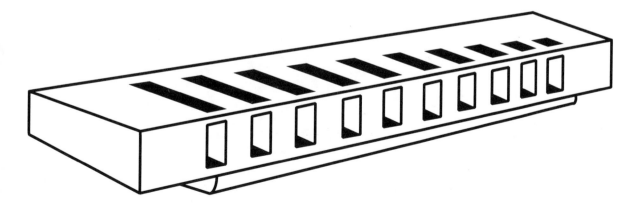

Harmonica reeds are tiny pieces of metal that vibrate when air is gently blown or drawn across them.

BREATHING

Playing the harmonica takes about as much breath as whistling a happy tune. If you find yourself running out of breath, stop and take a breather. Remember you're playing a wonderful musical instrument and not blowing up balloons. Relax. Don't blow too hard. Relax. Don't draw too hard. Relax.

AIMING YOUR BREATH

Right now you are probably blowing/drawing through several holes at a time. That's OK, because the harmonica was designed so that playing several holes at the same time will sound pretty good most of the time. This feature makes the harmonica very user friendly. As your playing get's better, you'll find your aim improving so that you can play three, two, and, ultimately, just one hole at a time. This is one way you can measure your progress as a harmonica player.

To aim your breath just pucker your lips as if you were whistling:

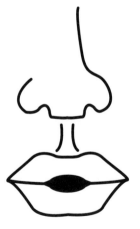

The size of your pucker will determine how many holes you blow/draw at the same time. With experience your aim will improve and you'll be able to play just one hole at a time.

WHAT IS THE SOUND OF ONE HOLE?

If your answer to this question is, "One whole what?" maybe you should sit down and take a breather. You've probably hyperventilated. Of course, the "hole" that we are talking about here is the beautiful sound of a single, lone tone played on the harmonica.

Until the ability to aim his breath settles in, *every* harmonica player starts out by playing several tones at the same time. So you're in good company.

In order for you to hear what one hole sounds like try this little experiment: Block all of the holes but one with your index fingers as shown in the illustration below. Gently blow or draw through the open hole between your fingers. Listen carefully to the beautiful single tone that you are playing. Try to remember everything that you can about that sound. Now, take your fingers away, and try to play that same beautiful tone again using your lips to aim your breath instead of your fingers.

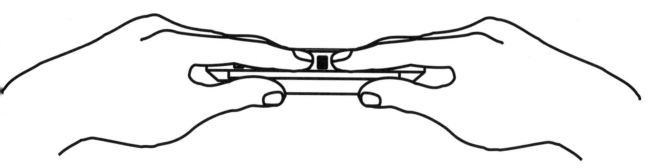

Playing beautiful tones one at a time is every harmonica player's ultimate goal. With this experiment you can hear what you're aiming at.

Try this simple experiment on each hole of your harmonica. In a short time it will be easy for you to aim your breath and play just two or three holes most of the time. Continue to work on narrowing your pucker, and your playing will soon be filled with the sound of beautiful single tones.

PLAYING SONGS

THE FASTEST WAY TO READ HARMONICA MUSIC

So far you've been having a great time playing around with your harmonica. Well, now you'll have even more fun as you start learning how to play some songs. And you'll be glad to know that playing a song on the harmonica isn't much harder than the "playing around" that you have been doing so far.

The biggest difference is that your playing will now be more focused. You'll be aiming at playing tones in a certain order to make a melody. If you have a very good ear for music you may have already picked out some simple melodies on your own. For most of us, however, some kind of written guide is needed so that we know exactly which holes to aim at and in what order to blow/draw them. The standard notation that is usually used for this can be very complex and difficult to read for beginners. In fact, for many people, trying to read standard notation is the hardest part about learning to play an instrument. Standard notation is also one of the main reasons why so many people *used* to take music lessons!

Well, in order to get started playing melodies on the harmonica *instantly* you DON'T HAVE TO READ STANDARD NOTATION! That's right, all you need to read to get started is a simple form of *tablature* that consists entirely of numbers and arrows:

tablature	means	play by
6↑	"blow 6"	blowing air into hole 6
5↑	"blow 5"	blowing air into hole 5
4↑	"blow 4"	blowing air into hole 4
4↓	"draw 4"	drawing air out of hole 4

This tablature is used throughout Instant Harmonica. *E-Z PLAY® notation will be used along with this tablature as you progress.*

TARGET PRACTICE...PREVIEWING THE TONES IN A SONG

At the beginning of each song in *Instant Harmonica* you will find an illustration like this one that will show you exactly what holes are used to play the tones for that song. Warm-up by doing some target practice on these tones before you try playing the song.

	1	2	3	4	5	6	7	8	9	10
blow				4↑	5↑	6↑				
draw				4↓						

MERRILY WE ROLL ALONG

5↑	4↓	3↑	4↓	5↑	5↑	5↑
Mer	- ri	- ly	we	roll	a	- long

4↓	4↓	4↓		5↑	6↑	6↑
Roll	a	- long		roll	a	- long

5↑	4↓	3↑	4↓	5↑	5↑	5↑
Mer	- ri	- ly	we	roll	a	- long

4↓	4↓	5↑	4↓	4↑
O'er	the	deep	blue	sea.

RHYTHM...THE LONG AND SHORT OF IT

In every song some tones are short, and some tones are long. The difference in the length of the tones is called *rhythm*. It is easy to play a song's rhythm if you sing the words in your head while you are playing the song on the harmonica.

YOU *CAN* BEAT THIS

You may already know that all music has a beat. Just as your heartbeat keeps you going, beat is vital to making music sound alive. Without a good beat, songs sound dead, even if everything else is played perfectly. Because it is so much a part of all of us, beat is one of the easiest concepts in music to understand. Whenever you have clapped, snapped or tapped along with a song you have played the beat. So, without even trying, you've already had years of practice keeping a steady beat. Well, don't stop now! Get in the habit of steadily tapping your foot every time you play the harmonica. If you're shy, it's all right to just wiggle your big toe. The important thing is that you *physically* feel the beat. Just like many other things in music, if you think about it too much you'll lose it. Just feel it and do it.

IT'S NOT MUCH TO LOOK AT

A picture of the beat would look like a series of evenly-spaced lines:

| | | | | | | | | | | | |

A steady pulse like this isn't very glamorous but it provides a solid foundation for making music. When you play the harmonica and you notice your listeners tapping their feet or clapping their hands, they are paying you one of the greatest compliments that anyone can give a musician. They are really getting into the music that you are making. You are literally moving them!

METER...MEASURING THE BEAT

Meter in music means that a song's beat is felt and counted in equal groups of two, three or four beats per group. These groups are called *measures* and the first beat of each measure is always *accented* like this:

| | | | | | | |
count: **1** 2 3 4 **1** 2 3 4

Of course, you can't count out loud and play the harmonica at the same time, but you can tap your foot and feel the accents. To help you get started, the next few songs will have the counts printed beneath the lyrics.

	1	2	3	4	5	6	7	8	9	10
blow			3↑	4↑	5↑					
draw				4↓	5↓					

GOODNIGHT LADIES

5↑		4↑		3↑	4↑		
Good		night		la	- dies		
1	2	3	4	1	2	3	4

5↑		4↑		4↓	4↓		
Good		night		la	- dies		
1	2	3	4	1	2	3	4

5↑		4↑		5↓	5↓		5↓
Good		night		la	- dies		We're
1	2	3	4	1	2	3	4

5↑	5↑	4↓	4↓	4↑			
Goin'	to	leave	you	now.			
1	2	3	4	1	2	3	4

TONGUE-TAPPING TECHNIQUE

Your tongue will help you play rhythms clearly on the harmonica. By saying *"ta"* when you play a tone, your tongue will tap against the roof of your mouth just behind your front teeth.

Try this exercise with any tone you like:

tongue:	**Ta**	**Ta**	**Ta**	**Ta**	**Ta**	**Ta**	**Ta**	**Ta**
count:	**1**	2	3	4	**1**	2	3	4

For longer tones use *"Toe-oe"* with your tongue tapping once for the *"Toe"* and then resting one *"oe"* for each additional beat that the tone is held:

tongue:	**Toe**	-	**oe**	**Toe**	-	**oe**	**Toe**	-	**oe**	-	**oe**	-	**oe**
count:	**1**		2	3		4	**1**		2		3		4

When you play more than one tone per beat use Ti Ti (Tea Tea):

tongue:	**Ti**	**Ti**	**Ti**	**Ti**	**Ti**	**Ti**	**Ti**	**Ti**	**Ti**	**Ti**	**Ti**	**Ti**	**Ti**	**Ti**	**Ti**	**Ti**
count:	**1**		2		3		4		**1**		2		3		4	

Of course, most songs use a combination of long and short tones like this:

tongue:	**Ta**	**Ta**	**Ti**	**Ti**	**Ta**	**Ta**	**Ta**	**Ti**	**Ti**	**Ta**	**To**	-	**oe**	-	**oe**	-	**oe**
count:	**1**	2	3			4	**1**	2	3		4		**1**	2		3	4

Now it's time to take a tongue-technique test by trying to tackle some tougher tonguing. The words have been omitted from the "Mystery Tune" on page 17. In place of the lyrics, you will find the rhythm syllables that you just learned. Take the time to play this melody with the correct rhythm using your best tongue-tapping technique and you'll have no trouble naming the title of this terrific tune.

	1	2	3	4	5	6	7	8	9	10
blow				4↑	5↑	6↑				
draw				4↓	5↓					

MYSTERY TUNE

4↑ 5↑ 5↓ 6↑   4↑ 5↑ 5↓ 6↑

Ta   ta   ta   toe- oe - oe - oe - oe   ta   ta   ta   toe - oe - oe - oe -
1   2   3   4   1   2   3   4   1   2   3   4   1   2   3   4

4↑ 5↑ 5↓ 6↑   5↑   4↑   5↑   4↓

oe   ta   ta   ta   toe- oe   toe- oe   toe - oe   toe- oe   toe- oe - oe - oe -
1   2   3   4   1   2   3   4   1   2   3   4   1   2   3   4

5↑ 5↑ 4↓ 4↑   4↑ 5↑   6↑ 6↑ 6↑ 5↓

oe   ta   ta   ta   toe- oe - oe   ta   toe - oe   ta   ta   ta   toe- oe - oe -
1   2   3   4   1   2   3   4   1   2   3   4   1   2   3   4

5↑ 5↑ 5↓ 6↑   5↑   4↑   4↓   4↑

oe   ta   ta   ta   toe   oe   oe   oe   oe   ta   ta   ta   toe   oe   oe   oe
1   2   3   4   1   2   3   4   1   2   3   4   1   2   3   4

WALTZES...THREE BEATS IN A MEASURE

Not every song that you play will have four beats per measure. The songs "Largo" and "Goodbye Old Paint" are examples of songs with three beats per measure.

"Largo" should be played *very* slowly and with much feeling. Be sure that you still keep a steady beat.

	1	2	3	4	5	6	7	8	9	10
blow				4↑	5↑	6↑				
draw				4↓						

LARGO

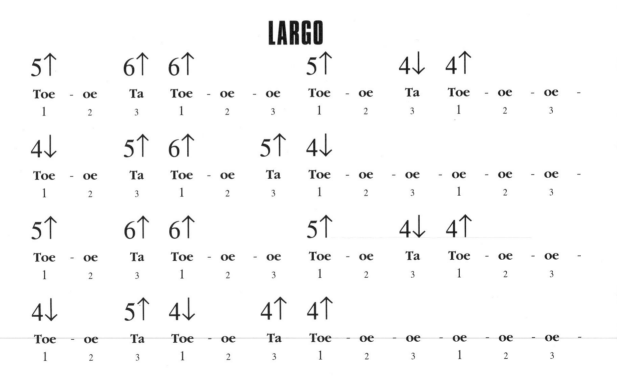

	1	2	3	4	5	6	7	8	9	10
blow				4↑	5↑	6↑				
draw				4↓		6↓				

GOODBYE OLD PAINT

6↓ 6↑   6↓ 4↑   6↓ 6↑ 5↑ 4↓
Good - bye   old Paint,   I'm leav - ing Chey-
1   2   3   1   2   3   1   2   3   1   2   3

4↑   6↓ 6↑   6↓ 4↑   6↓ 6↑ 5↑ 4↓ 4↑
enne.   Good - bye   old Paint,   I'm leav - ing Chey- enne.
1   2   3   1   2   3   1   2   3   1   2   3

6↑ 4↑ 4↑ 4↑ 4↑ 4↑ 4↑ 5↑ 4↓ 5↑ 4↓
My foot's in the stir rup, I'm off to Mon -
1   2   3   1   2   3   1   2   3   1   2   3

4↑   6↓ 6↑   6↓ 4↑   6↓ 6↑ 5↑ 4↓
tan'.   Good - bye   old Paint,   I'm leav - ing Chey -
1   2   3   1   2   3   1   2   3   1   2   3

4↑   6↓ 6↑   6↓ 4↑   6↓ 6↑ 5↑ 4↓ 4↑
enne.   Good - bye   old Paint,   I'm leav - ing Chey- enne
1   2   3   1   2   3   1   2   3   1   2   3   1   2   3

MUSICAL ABC'S

THE MUSICAL ALPHABET

Tones are given *pitch* names based on how high or low they sound. The seven letters of the *musical alphabet* (A B C D E F G) are used to name *all* of the tones used in music. The chart below shows the pitch name of every tone played on a C harmonica. The 15 tones used to play the songs in this book are bolder:

	1	2	3	4	5	6	7	8	9	10
blow ↑	C	E	**G**	**C**	**E**	**G**	**C**	**E**	**G**	**C**
draw ↓	D	G	**B**	**D**	**F**	**A**	**B**	**D**	**F**	**A**

WHAT A GUY!...THE INVENTOR OF THE MUSICAL STAFF

Since melodies move around from tone to tone, it would be very helpful to have some way of seeing the melodic shape. Well, a thousand years ago an Italian musician by the name of Guido d'Arezzo came up with the brilliant idea of writing notes on a series of lines and spaces to indicate the pitch of each tone. Guido's invention is called the staff. Here's how the tones used in this book look when their notes are placed on the musical staff:

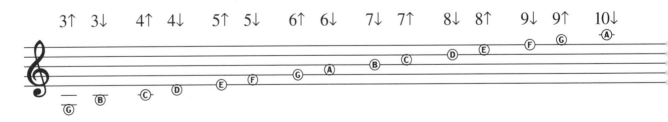

HERE'S HOW IT ALL WORKS

To help you see how Guido's invention works, here, again, is "Merrily We Roll Along," the first song that you learned, but this time it is written out using notes on a staff. The tablature still appears above the staff. Try to play through the song by reading the notation on the staff as well as the tablature. Using Guido's staff you can see as well as hear a melody's shape.

	1	2	3	4	5	6	7	8	9	10
blow				4↑	5↑	6↑				
draw				4↓						

MERRILY WE ROLL ALONG

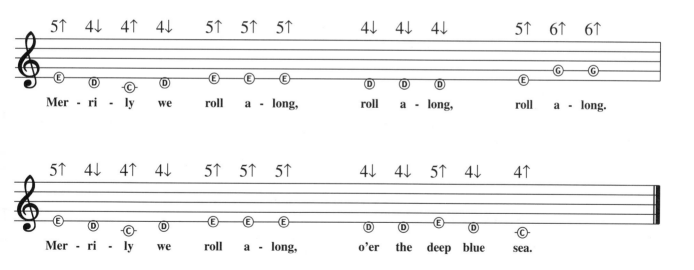

MORE STUFF ABOUT THE STAFF

When notes are printed on the musical staff, several other symbols are used both to save space and to let you quickly see how the notes are to be played:

Time Signature	This tells you the meter used in the song. The top number tells you how many beats are in each measure of the song.
Bar Lines	These vertical lines mark off each measure.
Double Bar Line	Marks the end of the song.

	1	2	3	4	5	6	7	8	9	10
blow				4↑	5↑	6↑				
draw				4↓	5↓	6↓				

MICHAEL, ROW THE BOAT ASHORE

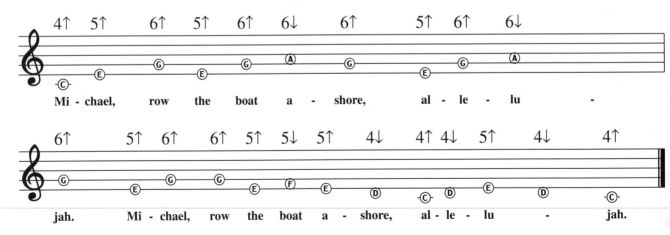

REAL NAMES FOR REAL NOTES

Where a note is written on the staff tells you its pitch (A, B, C, etc.). *How* a note is written tells you its rhythmic value (1 beat, 2 beats, etc.). This table reviews and names all of the long and short notes that you have played so far:

number of beats	4	3	2	1	1
written	○	♩.	♩	♩	♫
rhythm	Toe-oe-oe-oe	Toe-oe-oe	Toe-oe	Ta	Ti-ti
called	whole note	dotted half note	half note	quarter note	two eighth notes

PICKUP NOTES...LIFE BEFORE THE FIRST ONE

Many songs such as "When The Saints Go Marching In" (p. 17) and "Goodbye Old Paint" (p. 19) begin with what looks like a "short" measure. For example, although the time signatures for the next two songs indicate that each tune should have four-beat measures throughout, the first measures of these songs have fewer than four beats. The notes in these "short" measures are called pickup notes. Here's how to count the pickup notes:

	1	2	3	4	5	6	7	8	9	10
blow				4↑	5↑	6↑				
draw				4↓	5↓	6↓				

OH! SUSANNA

me, I've___ come from Al - a - bam - a with my ban - jo on my

knee. It ___ rained all night the day I left, the weath - er it was

dry, The ___ sun so hot I froze to death! Su - san - na don't you

cry. Oh! Su - san - na, Oh, don't you cry for

me, I've ___ come from Al - a - bam - a with my ban - jo on my knee.

TIES...TURNING TWO TONES INTO ONE

The curved lines connecting some of the notes in "Kumbaya" are called *ties*. Ties are used to show that the two tied notes should be played as one continuous tone equal in length to the two tied notes.

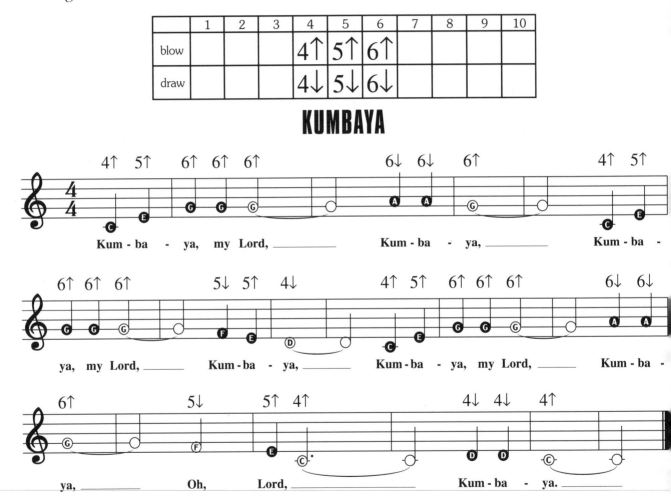

	1	2	3	4	5	6	7	8	9	10
blow				4↑	5↑	6↑				
draw				4↓	5↓	6↓				

KUMBAYA

RESTS...KNOWING WHEN *NOT* TO PLAY

An important part of every melody is the silence that occurs between some of the tones. These silences are called *rests*. Notes tell you to play a tone. Rests tell you *not* to play:

number of beats	4	3	2	1	1/2
written	▬	▬.	▬	≀	❜
called	*whole rest*	*dotted half rest*	*half rest*	*quarter rest*	*eighth rest*

ENDINGS..."PLAY IT AGAIN" AND "I'M OUTTA HERE!"

Not wanting to write out a long song with nearly identical sections, musicians have naturally devised a way of telling you to go back and play some or all of a song over again. They do this by using two different endings.

The first ending is used when you want to "play it again" and repeat the first part of the song. After repeating the first part of the song you move on to the second ending. This one has the same function as the phrase "I'm outta here," since it quickly takes you to the end of the song.

In "Act Naturally" the first ending sends you back to the beginning of the song to play the second verse. When you come to the endings the second time *skip the first ending* and go right on to the second ending where the song comes to an end.

	1	2	3	4	5	6	7	8	9	10
blow				4↑	5↑	6↑				
draw				4↓	5↓	6↓				

ACT NATURALLY

Words and Music by Vonie Morrison
and Johnny Russell

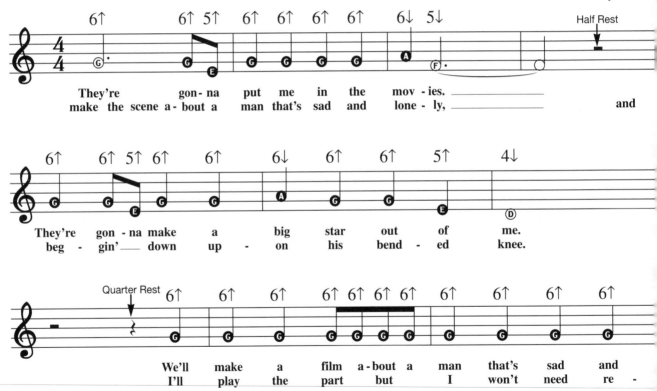

HIGH NOTES...MOVING RIGHT

To play the high tones in "Amazing Grace" move a little to the right on your harmonica:

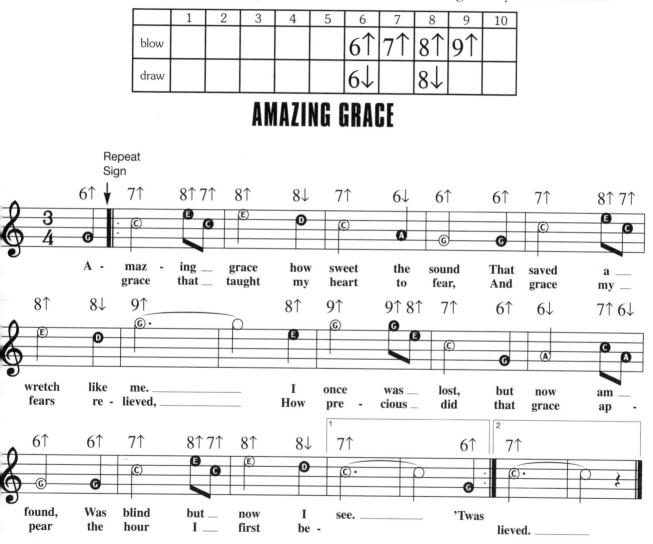

AMAZING GRACE

	1	2	3	4	5	6	7	8	9	10
blow				4↑	5↑	6↑	7↑			
draw				4↓	5↓	6↓				

DRINK TO ME ONLY WITH THINE EYES

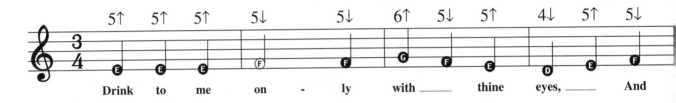

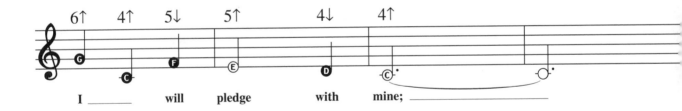

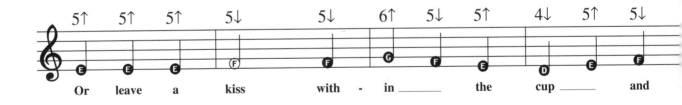

34

	1	2	3	4	5	6	7	8	9	10
blow				4↑	5↑	6↑	7↑			
draw				4↓	5↓	6↓	7↓			

CAMPTOWN RACES

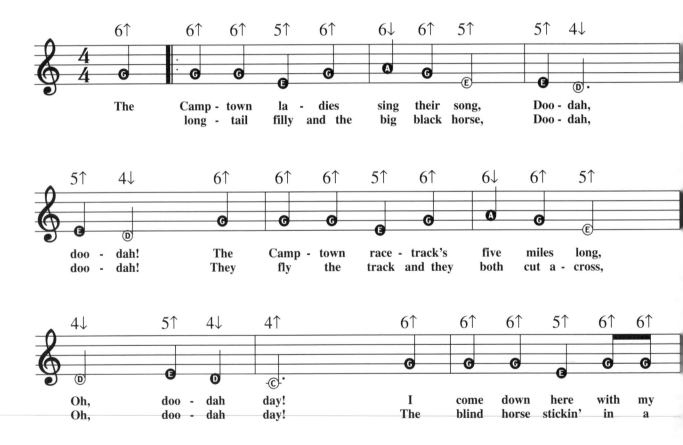

The Camp - town la - dies sing their song, Doo - dah,
long - tail filly and the big black horse, Doo - dah,

doo - dah! The Camp - town race - track's five miles long,
doo - dah! They fly the track and they both cut a - cross,

Oh, doo - dah day! I come down here with my
Oh, doo - dah day! The blind horse stickin' in a

BLUE NOTES

The blues and the harmonica are made for each other. It is relatively easy to get a great bluesy sound on the harmonica by *bending* tones, making them sound a little lower in pitch than they normally would. These "bent" tones are called *blue notes*. You bend a tone by blowing or drawing with a *little* more force than you would normally use. Tones that can be bent will be indicated with a bent arrow (♩ or ♪) in the tablature and a flat sign (♭) in the music. Feel free to try bending other tones if you think they will sound better than when they are played "straight." Remember that just a little extra force is needed to bend a tone. Don't overdo it.

	1	2	3	4	5	6	7	8	9	10
blow				4↑	5↑	6↑	7↑			
draw				4↓	5↓	6↓	7↓			

FRANKIE AND JOHNNY

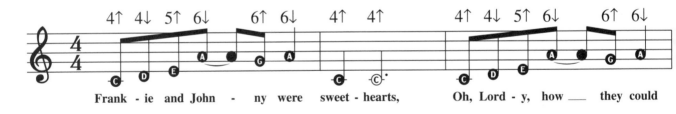

Frank - ie and John - ny were sweet - hearts,   Oh, Lord - y, how ___ they could

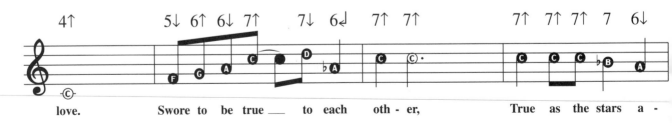

love.   Swore to be true ___ to each oth - er,   True as the stars a -

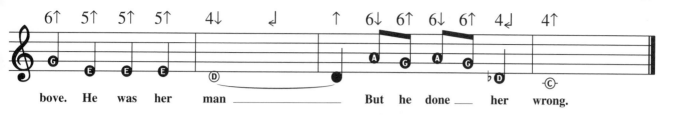

bove.　He　was　her　man　_____　But　he　done　___　her　wrong.

VIBRATOS...WAILING ON THE LONG TONES

Just like blue notes, *vibrato* is another great special effect that is characteristic of the harmonica's sound. Vibrato works best when it is used on long, plaintive notes like the ones found in "On Top Of Old Smoky" and "Down In The Valley." You can create the vibrato effect by using either your tongue or your right hand.

Tongue vibrato — Simply wiggle your tongue as you play a tone. The wiggling alters the air flow making the tone "wah-wah..." You can change the speed of the wah-wahs by changing the speed of your wiggle. Try starting out slowly, gradually increasing the speed of the vibrato and finally slowing down until you are back to a straight tone again.

Hand vibrato — This is a little more work than the tongue vibrato. In normal playing position your hands should be cupped around the harmonica with your left hand on top and your right hand on the bottom (lefties will have their right hand on top and left hand on the bottom). To play hand vibrato, start with your palms touching. Then start "flapping" your bottom hand as if it were a door hinged at your palms. As you play a long tone the tone will begin to "wah-wah" as it did when you wiggled your tongue. The faster you flap your hand the faster the vibrato will sound. Again, practice this technique by moving from slow to fast to slow on any long tone.

The long tones in "Down In The Valley" and "On Top Of Old Smoky" are perfect for trying out both kinds of vibrato.

	1	2	3	4	5	6	7	8	9	10
blow			3↑	4↑	5↑	6↑				
draw			3↓	4↓	5↓	6↓				

DOWN IN THE VALLEY

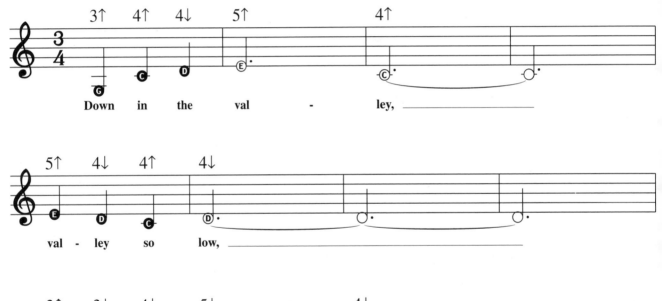

Down in the val - ley, _____

val - ley so low, _____

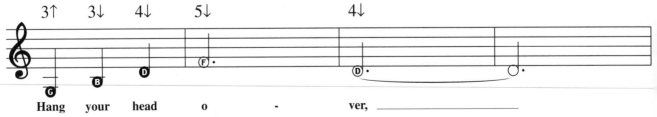

Hang your head o - ver, _____

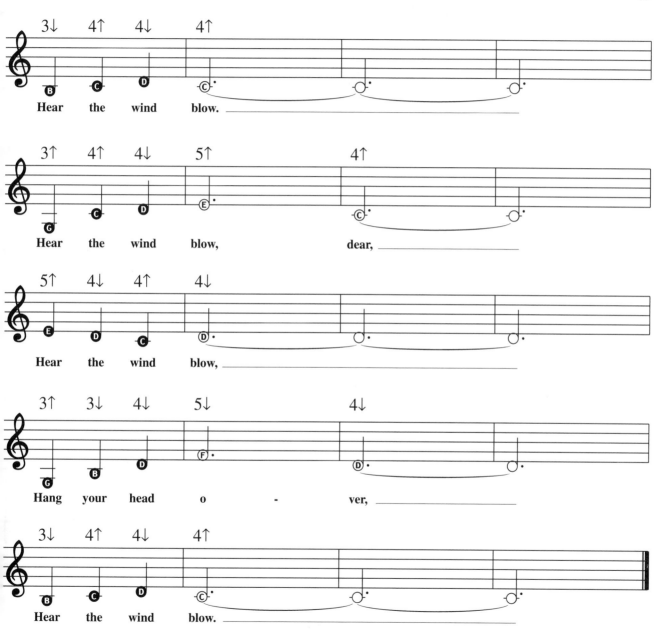

40

	1	2	3	4	5	6	7	8	9	10
blow				4↑	5↑	6↑	7↑			
draw				4↓	5↓	6↓	7↓			

ON TOP OF OLD SMOKY

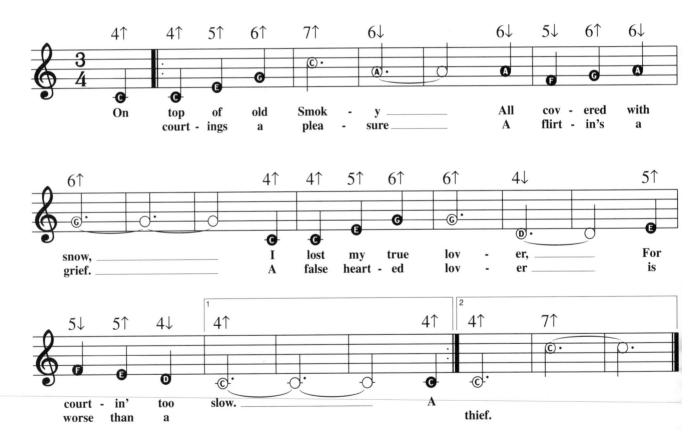

DOTTED NOTES...LONGER THAN THEY LOOK

Dotted half notes, like the ones in "On Top Of Old Smoky," are just one example of how placing a dot next to a note adds value (length) to that tone according to the following rule:

A dot placed next to any note always adds to that tone one half its value.

Here is how this rule works with half notes and quarter notes:

note	original value +	value of the dot	=	value of dotted note
♩	2 +	1	=	3
♩	1 +	1/2	=	1 1/2

Dotted quarter notes are usually grouped with a single eighth note. Together the dotted quarter note (1 1/2) and the eighth note (1/2) equal two beats:

play:	♩.			♪	♩		♩	
count:	1	and	2	and	3	and	4	and
feel:	long		-	short	long		long	

In "Home Sweet Home," on the next page, this rhythm pattern is used five times. Be sure that each of these has a long-short feel.

	1	2	3	4	5	6	7	8	9	10
blow				4↑	5↑	6↑	7↑			
draw				4↓	5↓	6↓	7↓			

HOME SWEET HOME

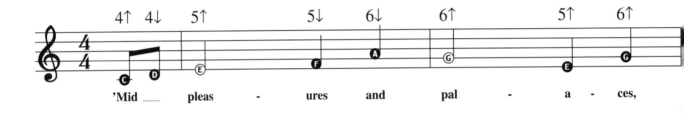

'Mid — pleas - ures and pal - a - ces,

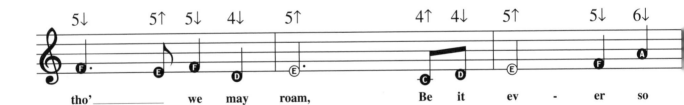

tho' we may roam, Be it ev - er so

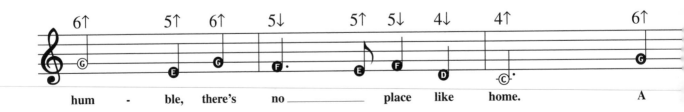

hum - ble, there's no place like home. A

43

44

	1	2	3	4	5	6	7	8	9	10
blow			3↑	4↑	5↑	6↑				
draw			3↓	4↓	5↓					

STREETS OF LAREDO

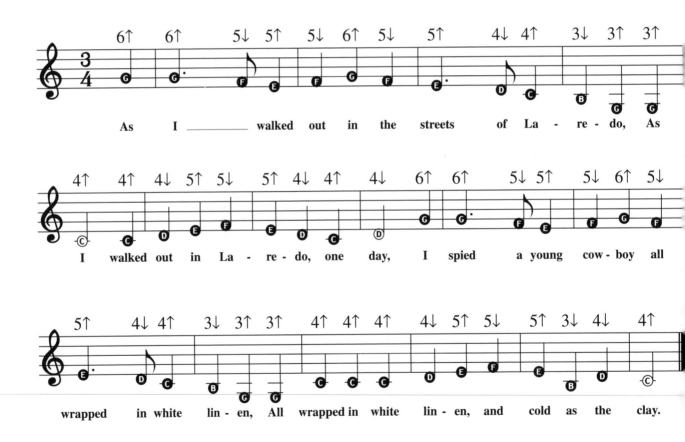

	1	2	3	4	5	6	7	8	9	10
blow				4↑	5↑	6↑				
draw			3↓	4↓	5↓	6↓				

BLOW THE MAN DOWN

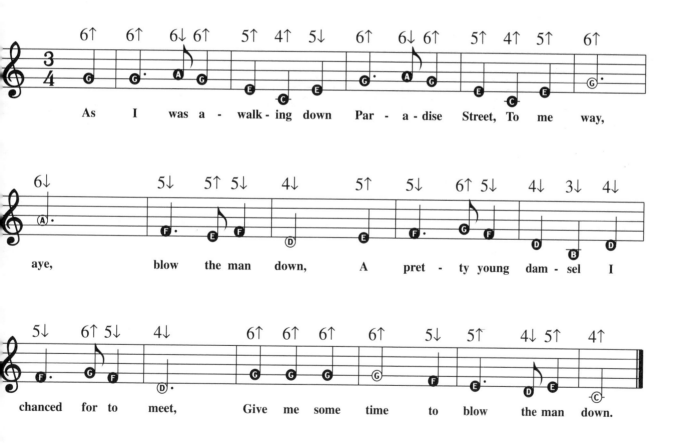

46

	1	2	3	4	5	6	7	8	9	10
blow					5↑	6↑	7↑	8↑		
draw						6↓	7↓	8↓		

MY BONNIE LIES OVER THE OCEAN

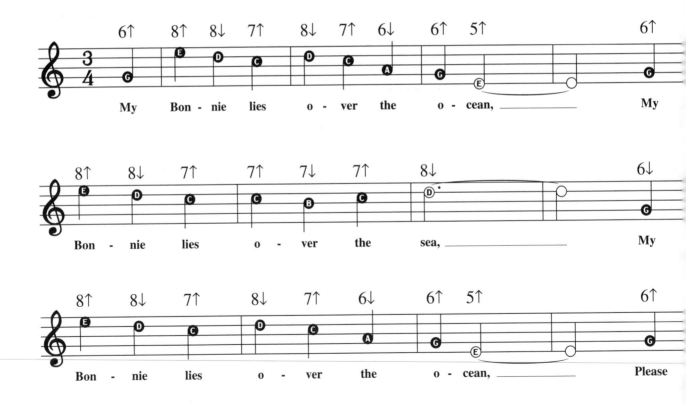

	1	2	3	4	5	6	7	8	9	10
blow				4↑	5↑	6↑				
draw			3↓	4↓	5↓	6↓				

OKIE FROM MUSKOGEE

Words and Music by Merle Haggard
and Roy Edward Burris

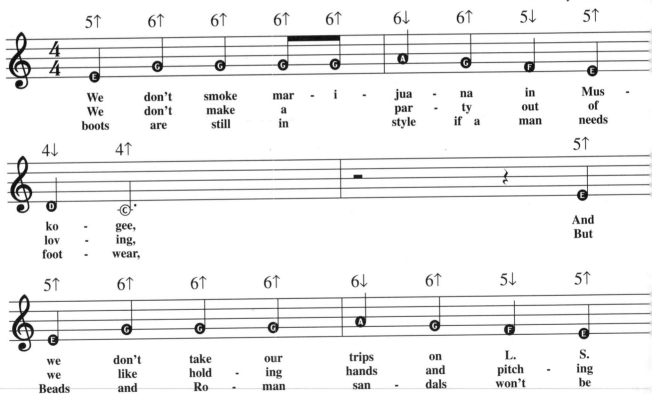

50

D-I-V-O-R-C-E

Words and Music by Bobby Braddock
and Curly Putman

CODAS...MUSIC'S "TAIL"

The first time that you play "Where Does The Good Times Go" you may be asking yourself: "Where do I go from here?" The reason for your confusion is probably the *Coda*. Codas (Italian for "tail") are always found at the end of a song. But, how do you get there from here? You get to the coda by following the directions printed in the music. The first direction appears in Italian at the end of the second ending, D.C. al Coda, followed by an English translation "Return to beginning, Play to ⊕ and Skip to Coda." So you play the song again through measure 14 where you find the Coda sign (⊕) with the words "To Coda." From there skip ahead to the Coda and end the song.

	1	2	3	4	5	6	7	8	9	10
blow						6↑	7↑	8↑		
draw						6↓	7↓	8↓	9↓	

WHERE DOES THE GOOD TIMES GO

Words and Music by
Buck Owens

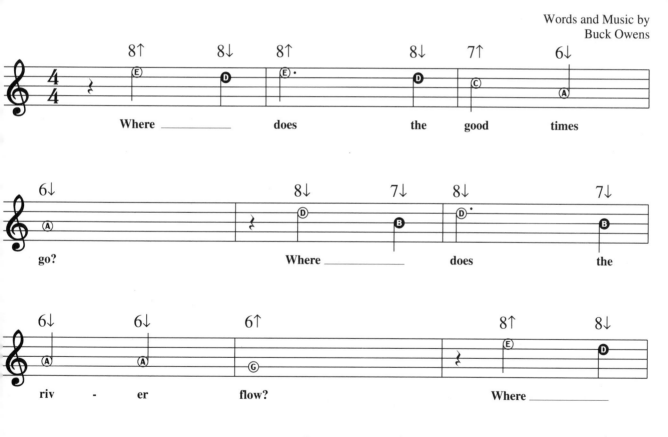

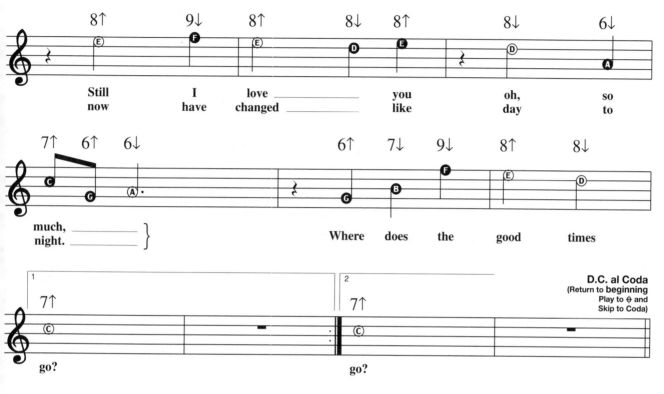

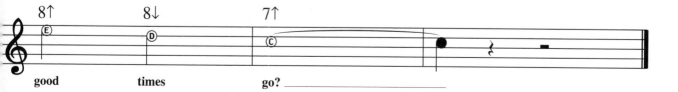

	1	2	3	4	5	6	7	8	9	10
blow				4↑	5↑	6↑	7↑			
draw				4↓	5↓	6↓	7↓			

SWEET BETSY FROM PIKE

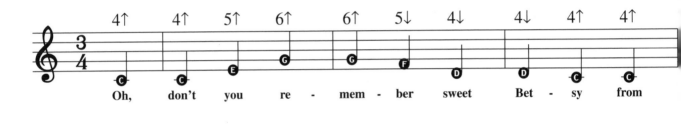

Oh, don't you re - mem - ber sweet Bet - sy from

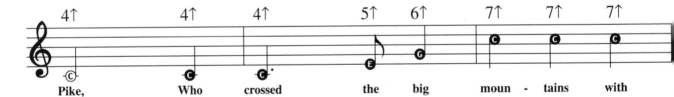

Pike, Who crossed the big moun - tains with

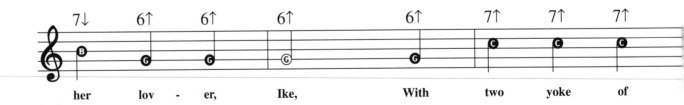

her lov - er, Ike, With two yoke of

59

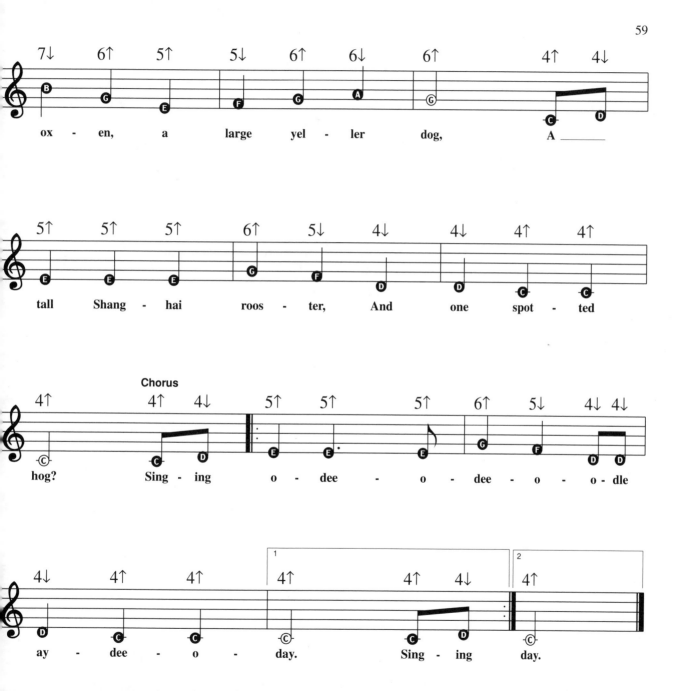

FOLLOW THE SIGNS

Remember what a Coda is? In "Ocean Front Property" you'll find a new way of getting to it. Instead of the instructions *D.C. al Coda* (return to the beginning, then to the Coda), in the second ending of "Ocean Front Property" you are told D.S. al Coda (Return to 𝄋 Play to ⊕ and skip to Coda). The big difference is that instead of going all the way back to the beginning of the song (D.C.) you return to the sign (𝄋). In this case you'll find the sign at the end of measure 16. Just as you did in "Where Do The Good Times Go," you will play from there until you come to the Coda sign (⊕ To Coda) at the beginning of the 1st ending. From there skip to the Coda and end the song.

TRIPLETS...THREE TO A BEAT

As you might guess by their name, triplets come in threes. So far you have always played two eighth notes to a beat. In measure 13 of "Ocean Front Property" you will play three eighth notes to a beat. Here's how to count this measure:

play:	♩		♩		rest		♪	♪	♪
count:	1	and	2	and	3	and	4	and	a
lyrics:	love		you.				And	now	if

	1	2	3	4	5	6	7	8	9	10
blow				4↑	5↑	6↑	7↑			
draw				4↓	5↓	6↓	7↓			

OCEAN FRONT PROPERTY

Words and Music by Hank Cochran,
Dean Dillon and Royce Porter

62

63

	1	2	3	4	5	6	7	8	9	10
blow			3↑	4↑	5↑	6↑				
draw			3↓	4↓	5↓	6↓				

THE GAMBLER

Words and Music by
Don Schlitz

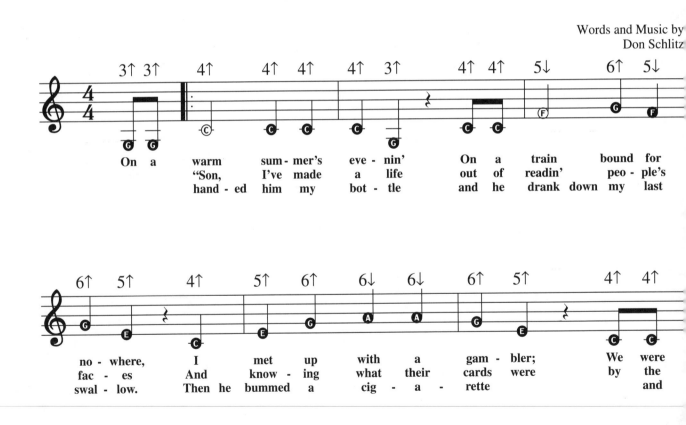

On a warm sum - mer's eve - nin' On a train bound for
"Son, I've made a life out of readin' peo - ple's
hand - ed him my bot - tle and he drank down my last

no - where, I met up with a gam - bler;
fac - es And know - ing what their cards were
swal - low. Then he bummed a cig - a - rette

We were by the
and

65

66

68

	1	2	3	4	5	6	7	8	9	10
blow						6↑	7↑	8↑	9↑	
draw						6↓	7↓	8↓	9↓	

GREEN GREEN GRASS OF HOME

Words and Music by
Curly Putman

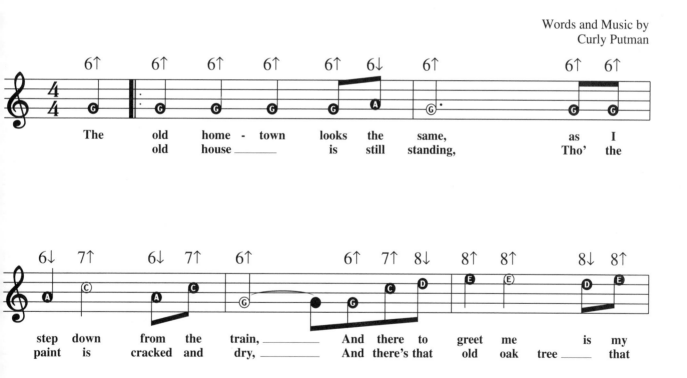

HOME ON THE RANGE

73

	1	2	3	4	5	6	7	8	9	10
blow			3↑	4↑	5↑	6↑	7↑			
draw				4↓	5↓	6↓		8↓		

SO YOU THINK YOU'RE A COWBOY

Words and Music by Hank Cochran
and Willie Nelson

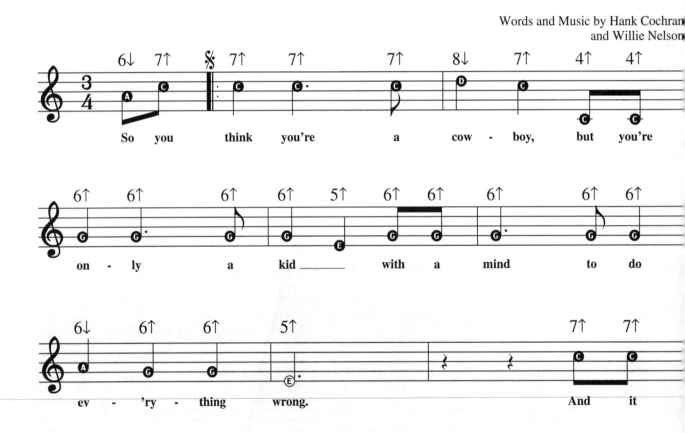

So you think you're a cow - boy, but you're on - ly a kid with a mind to do ev - 'ry - thing wrong. And it

76

	1	2	3	4	5	6	7	8	9	10
blow						6↑	7↑	8↑	9↑	
draw						6↓	7↓	8↓	9↓	10↓

BURY ME BENEATH THE WILLOWS

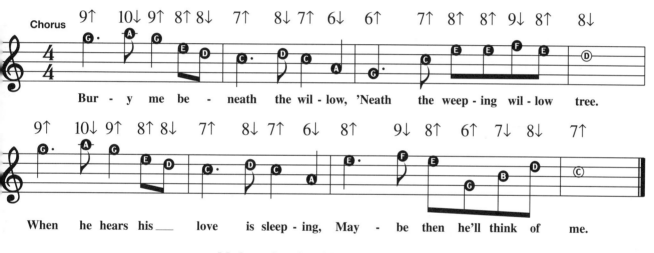

My heart is sad and I am lonely,
Thinking of the one I love.
When will I meet him? Oh, no never,
Unless we meet in heaven above.
To Chorus

Tomorrow was to be our wedding,
I pray, oh Lord, where can he be?
He's gone, he's gone to love another;
He no longer cares for me.
To Chorus

He told me that he dearly loved me,
How could I believe him untrue?
Until one day some neighbors told me.
"He has proven untrue to you."
To Chorus

	1	2	3	4	5	6	7	8	9	10
blow				4↑	5↑	6↑	7↑	8↑		
draw					5↓	6↓		8↓		

SOME DAYS ARE DIAMONDS

(SOME DAYS ARE STONE)

Words and Music by
Dick Feller

When you ask how I've been _____ here with - out you,

I like to say I've been fine and I do.

But we both know the truth is hard to come by,

79

TRIPLETS AND THEN SOME

When you learned "Ocean Front Property" you played one lonely set of triplets. Take a look at "Busted" and you might wonder why the song isn't called "Triplets." Don't let this song bust you, just take it at a nice slow pace. Since there are so many triplets you might even try counting in 12 instead of 4 like this:

play:	♩		♪	♪	♪	♪	♪	♪	♪	♪	♪	♪	♪	♪
feel:			1	2	3	4	5	6	7	8	9	10	11	12
count:	4	and	a	1	and	a	2	and	a	3	and	a	4	and	a
lyrics:	My		bills	are	all	due	and	the	ba -	by	needs	shoes	and	I'm

The "then some" in "Busted" are called sixteenth notes. Sixteenth notes are twice as fast (or, if you prefer, half as long) as eighth notes. Four sixteenths equal one beat and are usually counted like this:

play:	♪	♪	♪	♪	♪	♪	♪	♪	♪	♪	♪	♪	♪
count:	1	a	and	a	2	and	a	3	and	a	4	and	a
lyrics:	coun-ty's	gon - na	haul	my	be - long - ings		a - way	'cause	I'm

Whether you are playing triplets, sixteenths, or any other rhythm, always be sure that the beat (numbers) remains steady.

	1	2	3	4	5	6	7	8	9	10
blow				4↑	5↑	6↑	7↑			
draw				4↓	5↓	6↓	7↓			

BUSTED

Words and Music by
Harlan Howard

6↑ %5↑ 4↑ 4↑ 4↑ 6↑ 6↑ 5↑ 4↑ 4↑ 5↑ 4↓ 5↑

My bills are all due and the ba - by needs shoes and I'm
I   am   no thief but a man can go wrong when he's

5↓ 4↓ 5↓ 8↓ 8↓ 8↓ 8↓ 6↑ 6↑ 8↓ 8↓ 8↓ 7↓ 6↑ 6↑

bust - ed. The Cot - ton is down to a quart - er a pound and I'm
bust - ed. The food that we canned last sum - mer is gone and I'm

6↓ 5↑ 6↑ 6↑ 6↑ 5↑ 4↑ 4↑ 4↑ 6↑ 6↑ 5↑ 4↑ 4↑ 5↑ 6↑

bust - ed. I got a cow that's gone dry and a hen that won't lay, a
bust - ed. The fields are all bare and the cot - ton won't grow.

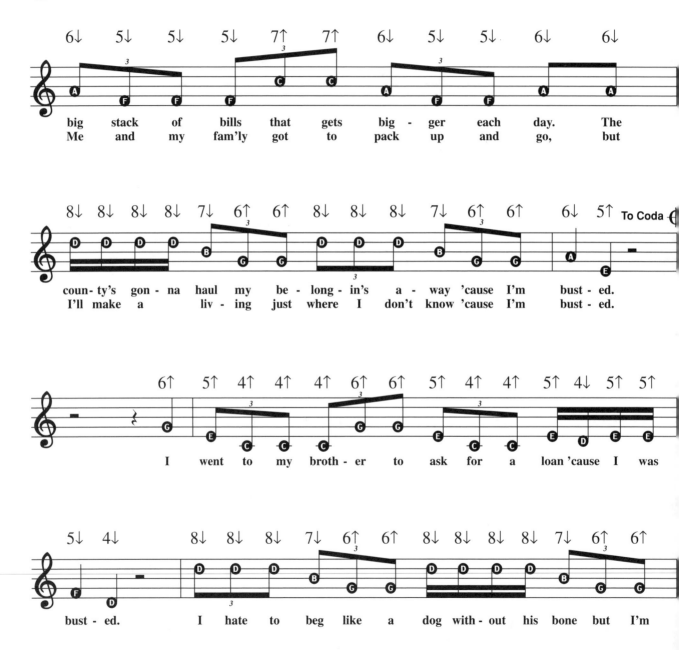

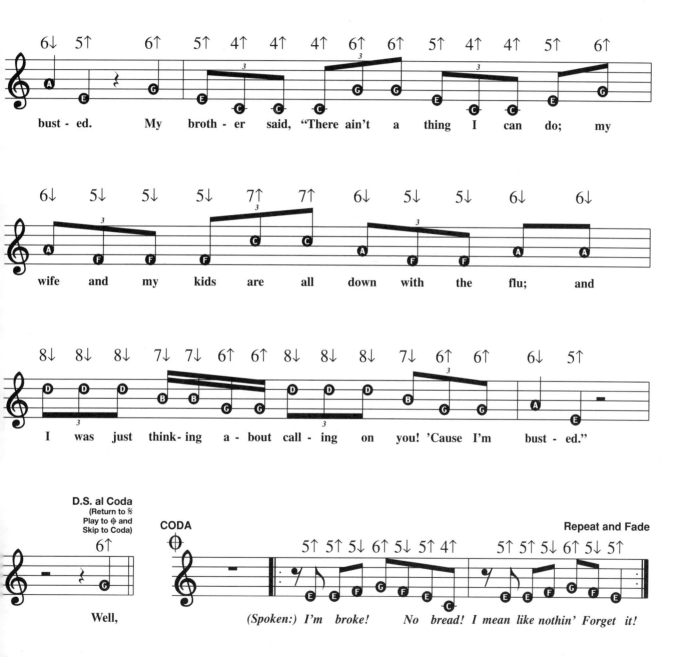

	1	2	3	4	5	6	7	8	9	10
blow				4↑	5↑	6↑	7↑			
draw			3↓	4↓	5↓	6↓	7↓			

MAKE THE WORLD GO AWAY

By Hank Cochran

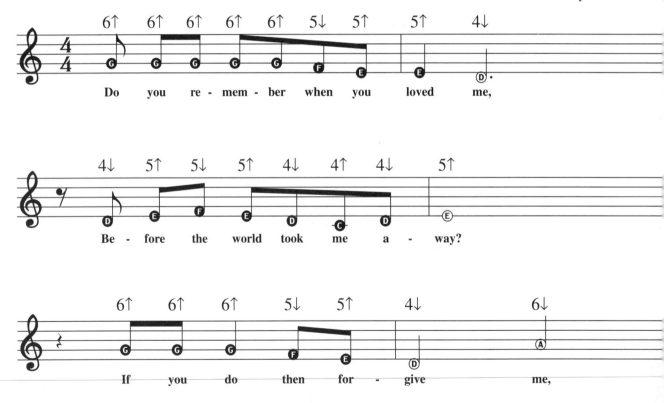

Do you re-mem-ber when you loved me,

Be - fore the world took me a - way?

If you do then for - give me,

	1	2	3	4	5	6	7	8	9	10
blow				4↑	5↑	6↑	7↑			
draw				4↓	5↓	6↓	7↓	8↓		

I'VE GOT A TIGER BY THE TAIL

Words and Music by Buck Owens
and Harlan Howard

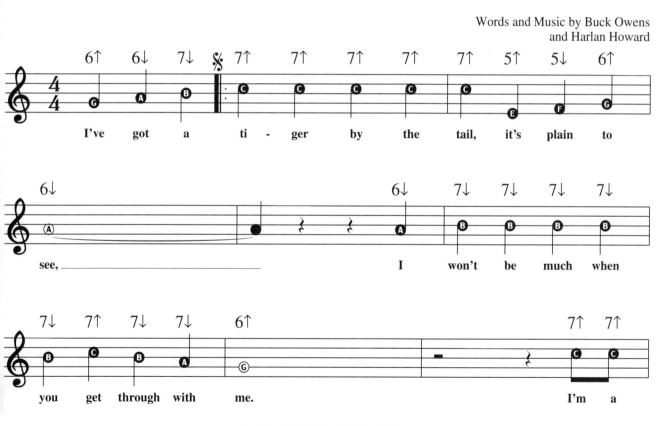

	1	2	3	4	5	6	7	8	9	10
blow				4↑	5↑	6↑	7↑			
draw				4↓	5↓	6↓	7↓	8↓		

OLD FOLKS AT HOME

(SWANEE RIVER)

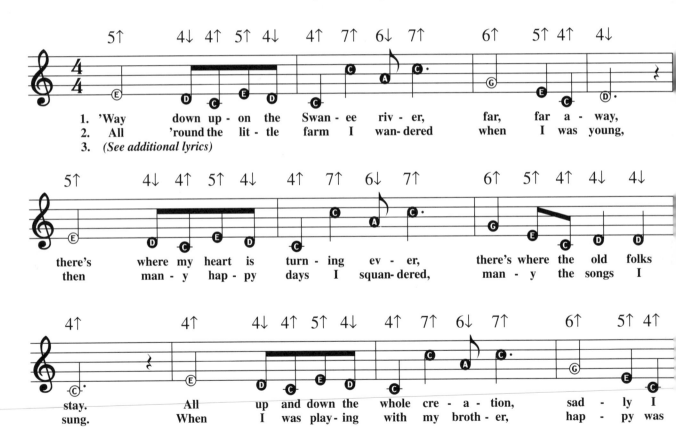

Additional Lyrics

3. One little hut among the bushes,
   One that I love,
   Still sadly to my mem'ry rushes,
   No matter where I rove.
   When will I see the bees a-humming
   All round the comb?
   When will I hear the banjo strumming
   Down in my good old home?

SHE'S GOT YOU

Words and Music by
Hank Cochran

93

THE TIP OF MY FINGERS

Words and Music by
Bill Anderson

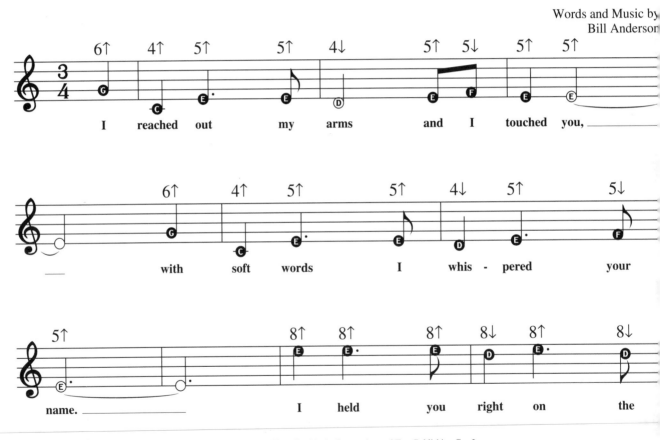